# COACHING COACH FOR SUCCESS

*How to unlock answers using powerful questions and achieving your life goals!*

*by*

*Tom Mahalo*

©Copyright 2016 All rights reserved.

This document is geared towards providing exact and reliable information in regards to the topic and issue covered. The publication is sold on the idea that the publisher is not required to render an accounting, officially permitted, or otherwise, qualified services. If advice is necessary, legal or professional, a practiced individual in the profession should be ordered.

From a Declaration of Principles which was accepted and approved equally by a Committee of the American Bar Association and a Committee of Publishers and Associations.

In no way is it legal to reproduce, duplicate, or transmit any part of this document by either electronic means or in printed format. Recording of this publication is strictly prohibited and any storage of this document is not allowed unless with written permission from the publisher. All rights reserved.

The information provided herein is stated to be truthful and consistent, in that any liability, in terms of inattention or otherwise, by any usage or abuse of any policies, processes, or directions contained within is the solitary and utter responsibility of the recipient reader. Under no circumstances will any legal responsibility or blame be held against the publisher for any reparation, damages, or monetary loss due to the information herein, either directly or indirectly. Respective authors own all copyrights not held by the publisher.

The information herein is offered for informational purposes solely and is universal as so. The presentation of the information is without the contract or any type of guarantee assurance.

The trademarks that are used are without any consent, and the publication of the trademark is without permission or backing by the trademark owner. All trademarks and brands within this book are for clarifying purposes only and are the owned by the owners themselves, not affiliated with this document.

# Table of Contents

Introduction .................................................................. 6

The power of coaching ............................................. 10

Being a positive coach .............................................. 17

Rhetorical questions ................................................. 25

"simple" questions .................................................... 33

Making simple questions matter ............................. 37

Neutral questions ...................................................... 41

The threat of interrogation ...................................... 48

!!!Bonus!!!Neurolinguistic programming ............ 55

Conclusion ................................................................. 78

# **Introduction**

First off, thank you for taking the time to download this guide on coaching!

My name is Tom Mahalo, and I've been lucky enough to have been involved in the development and application of sound coaching practices for a long period of time. Over the years I have been lucky enough to have worked with students who are interested in learning and engaging in a bid to find an easy, effective way to work.

It's this dedication to finding the right solution that has always been so exceptionally important to me – and it is what has driven me to write this guide. The world of coaching is a hard thing to get right and this is built for any coaches out there who want to improve their technique and who want to make sure that their clients and patients are going to be happier about opening up about what they have seen and experienced in life so far.

This is a huge thing to get involved with in your life, and with the right approach and mentality you should have no problems at all in making this a possibility if you use the right methods. This is why I have written this book; with the intention of helping readers get more controlled routes towards exploring the minds of their clients.

This should be a major talking point moving forward, as it will play a leading role in determining just how successful – or not – you are likely to be moving forward with your plans and your ambitions. Worried that your coaching ambitions might be stifled by an inability to get the right answers? Scared that a patient is going to go elsewhere as they cannot get the help that they need from you? Then this book is for you!

I have created every single part in here to make sure that you can fully understand and appreciate the challenges that lie ahead in coaching.

With this as your guide, you should have no problems in making those challenging elements of coaching become far more simplistic in its management. Now you'll spend less time trying to find solutions and more time implementing them. Instead of being railroaded and held back by problem along the way you can find that engaging with the right kind of questions can be the best way to get the level of results you are interested in.

This can be the catalyst that helps you finally move onto the next level as a coach, helping both yourself and your patients grow and develop.

So, does this sound like the kind of training and ideals that your own coaching practice has so heavily lacked in recent years? If so, it's time to make a progressive and long-term change to the way that you go about you're coaching.

The power of coaching and the elements of success that it can unlock in anyone is something that you should never discount, and with this book you'll learn how to manipulate the power of coaching and make sure that your future as a coach is going to be built on helping people find the results that they need!

# The Power of Coaching

When it comes to changing and improving lives, there are few better solutions out there to pick from than coaching. It is one of the most influential and useful situations that anyone can turn to, giving them the help that they need in discovering major changes about themselves and beyond.

Not only is the power of coaching something worth learning and understanding, but it's something that many coaches fail to actually use properly – how? Because they go about it the wrong way entirely, coaching with fear instead.

The power of coaching only exists when you learn that coaching is only successful through positivity. In a later section of the book, *Open Ended Questions* we will look together at the importance of giving people a choice when they are being coached. The power of coaching is this – you are expected to give people the path to find answers, not the answers.

A bad coach gives people the answers, as it shows they cannot coach. If you want to train someone then give them the answers and tell them to repeat it. If you would like someone to learn from scratch and eventually be able to do the job themselves, though? Then you need to coach and you need to understand the immense gravity of power that being a coach can have on a student.

So long as you use the power of coaching to make them think, you are on the right path.

When a coach is giving the student a chance to learn and to think for themselves, they are opening the chance for the student to become more aware of the situation moving forward. They'll be able to express themselves more and tell the coach what they think and what they feel. Whilst we'll discuss later the importance of doing this through positive, not negative, questioning it's important to note it right now as well.

The very essence of a good, strong coach is that they let the student look at their main strengths, not their glaring weaknesses.

This type of coach will make sure that the response from the student is the most powerful addition you can have – it will be personal. It comes from their own mind, not a textbook and not an online article they read. It's how they genuinely feel right now.

A good coach will take a value from learning about how a student feels. It should create a dialogue that means the student can talk for as long as they feel comfortable, never forcing timed answers and pressurized dynamics.

A good coach will always want to build up situational responses, sure, but it's all about putting the student in a position whereby they need to discover and learn the answer on their own. There are few better ways to learn and become a more accomplished person than through coaching, as it pushes the boundaries and opens up brand new opportunities.

## Using the Power

As we mentioned above, any coach worth their talent will be capable of helping the student find the answer, not give them it flat out. It needs to leave the student with at least a choice of answers to discuss and talk about, as most students are not quite sure of the real answer.

Therefore you have to be the guiding light that discusses these elements with the student so that they feel comfortable with what you are asking of them. A failure to do this means that responses become more canned and less personal, and therefore it will soon be much harder to coach that child.

However, one thing I want to make clear is that this is not always the case – it depends on the student, what they know, and how they respond. Some students need you to help them out in the beginning with more closed-end questions that have pre-destined answers.

Others will need you to do this at the end of the coaching as it allows them to be more focused on the points they suffer from the most in their repertoire. It's all about working these little elements out with your students.

Using the power of coaching, though, means that you use the power of positivity. Many students come to you as they feel like they cannot learn or are unable to do so elsewhere. You have to forge an environment that means they can sit down and learn with you, engaging their mind and giving them confidence in their own strength and capabilities.

You can only coach someone if they believe that they can be coached and this is what makes the power of coaching itself so unique – it needs to be fueled by the energy of positivity and power of progress.

Remember that a strong coach is all about giving someone the right kind of questioning. Whilst you should always stray towards positive ended questions, many students can struggle massively with the "pressure" of a closed end question. It leaves them feeling like they are back in school and need to answer fast.

This is why you need to remove the atmosphere of competition, and of failure. You are both here to learn together and to go through a process as a team, they are not here to appease your ego or to fill out your own criteria alone. No, a student is there to be infused by your power – your power of positivity, of truth and of education.

Keep this in mind as you move forward as a good coach will need to make the most of these elements if they wish to ensure that people are interested, invigorated and truly engaged by the techniques and the training that a good coach can provide them with.

Now, let's look at how you go about being a positive coach. It's well and good knowing that this is what you need to do, but how do you condition coaching to be like this?

# Being a Positive Coach

The hardest part of being a coach is being a positive one. Positivity is a hard thing to fake or create, so if you are not a naturally positive person you will undoubtedly have a harder time getting people to turn to you and appreciate your style of coaching.

A positive coach will always have a stronger and more productive bond with the students than one who tries to either coach through fear or coach through condescension. Many coaches use their superior knowledge and platform to talk down to and patronize students until they feel they are "on their level".

If you want to have a short career as a coach then by all means, do this!

The best coaches, though, coach by being friendly and positive.

*A prominent example of this comes from my own experience in sporting history. I used to play amateur football/soccer and I worked under a coach at these stages who was excellent. He was exceptionally positive, and the reason he was so good with the players is because he told us things like "When you run by your opponent" or "By the time you complete that pass".*

*To the normal person this might sound like nothing, and at the time it just seemed the norm. Our performances were excellent and the team had great chemistry. We were like a finely tuned business, with our coach dishing out the advice and the positivity even in the face of defeat.*

*Eventually, the coach moved on and he was replaced by a new coach who was supposed to be a more disciplinarian type. He came in and within the first few days had ripped through each member of the team for their "failure" to do specific parts of the game right. We went from being told we were just a bit of confidence short of being a top player to being told that, even on our best day, we weren't good enough for the top teams in the division.*

*Naturally, performances evaporated and players stopped progressing. Why? Because we believed the coach. We felt like we were no longer as good as we previously thought. Whilst both are arguably artificial – we were never as good as was claimed by our first coach, but never as bad as the second coach – we performed at more consistent, high levels with the positive frame of mind than negative.*

Not only does this create a unique and interesting little dilemma for a coach, but it sets the tone for coaches as well. You might think that a member of your team – sports, business or otherwise – is letting you down and isn't good enough at what you need them to be good at.

However, you will never see them improve and change that by being negative and reminding them about their quality (or lack of) as it will merely make them more conscious. You tell someone they suck enough and, before long, they will start to believe what you're saying!

**Engaging with Positivity**

As we mentioned above, no coach on this earth gets by long-term – and sees consistent improvement from their students – by managing with negativity and fear. It can work at first to get a group of underperformers back to the average, but you'll rarely get the act of fear to make sure they perform above and beyond.

Whilst there are always exceptions to prove the rule, it takes a very specific and experienced makeup of individuals to thrive in this kind of atmosphere. Those who are still learning or don't have this kind of steely resolve will fail.

As a coach, it's your duty to look beyond the dog eat dog world of results – again, in business and in any other walk of life – and look at the development. You might still not be hitting your targets as a coach and student grouping but so long as you can see a gradual progression then it's worth the time to stay positive.

Positivity will ensure that your students feel like they are making progress, and gives them the confidence and the energy to just get on with it. It stops them from doubting themselves and from looking back and feeling like they aren't achieving anything.

Take the time to get to do this right and you'll find that the act of engaging with positivity is a far simpler pursuit.

Indeed, being able to successfully engage with positivity is a really tough thing to do if you aren't that kind of person. However, it is an absolutely vital attribute for anyone who wants to see consistent and regular gains from all of their students.

Scared that this might not work in the future for you? Then you don't have enough positive engagement. Any coach who even goes through a week or being positive to their students, even in the face of failure or regression, will see a wholesale change in the attitude around the place.

Students are more likely to want to learn and they are going to be much more involved with the idea of helping clients make choices. Make sure that any questions you ask for are asked in the right time – use pre-emptive discussion to learn if the student has either already made a subconscious decision or whether they are fully ready to make that decision.

It's easier to coach when the student feels ready than forcing it, for sure.

The major benefit of doing this is that it will leave your client with a far more effective endgame. Sure, you could use specific questions to guide your client in the direction of a particular conclusion because you see it as the right one or because you are beginning to lack patience, but this is a pretty terrible way to treat a student.

No, your job here is to make sure that your students are simply moving towards the path of finding that conclusion on their own – don't try and push them towards something you find that suits your agendas. The worst thing you can do is use the wrong kind of questioning to make them think negatively, with the idea of using your coaching to fix that and fill in the answers to make them see you as the guru.

Now, let's take a look at different forms of questioning and why they matter so much.

# **Rhetorical Questions**

As a coach you need to be ready to ask different kinds of questions and different styles of questions to make sure that you get all the details that you could possibly need about each and every one of your students.

A failure to do this will make it quite hard for you to really appreciate what they are telling you, and more worryingly it will make it much harder to actually coach them and lead them in the right direction.

Sound like a fear you've got? Then consider rhetorical questions as a valid line of questioning for your students.

Rhetorical questions are mightily useful for a wide range of reasons, mainly because they look to elicit some form of approval so that the person you are talking to can understand what you are about to discuss or demonstrate. They are not "real" questions but they help you to set the agenda, designed to help you fully appreciate your direction.

Rhetorical questions are not typically very good coaching questions, and it's important that you take this into account. Outside of very particular topics and styles of coaching, this won't work!

Accidentally Rhetorical

A common mistake to make is to keep talking to someone and asking questions that aren't supposed to be rhetorical, whilst treating them as much. Many coaches naturally are quite charismatic and can get caught up in the sound of their own voices, making it easy for the choice to ask questions that need an answer, whilst already having the answer they would expect in their minds.

From there, they can just go on and make it harder for the student to stick with the agenda of the question itself. Not only is the pre-determined answer likely to be nothing to do with the client but it won't let them learn anything. They are now merely listening to the coaches' opinion on what they think of this particular answer – that is the worst kind of coaching that you can possibly hand out, and will significantly weaken your hand.

Basically, you need to work out if the question is actually worth asking in the first place. When you go to ask it, are you looking to open it up to be a debate or are you just looking to make a point? If it's the former then you should not have an answer ready, it should have to be made to fit with the answer provided by the student.

Sadly, too many couches take this approach and go with the latter – they ask questions thinking it makes them sound more engaging, but usually means the student just stops listening.

**Avoiding the Rhetoric**

Therefore, a good coach will only use rhetorical questions when they are asked to explain something that needs them as part of the explanation. Rhetorical questions should never be a primary or prominent part of your coaching as it is simply too generic. You don't actually know if what you are suggesting to the client is going to be suitable as the rhetorical question is universal, expecting the same answer to apply to everyone. This is an easy way to make a student doubt you're coaching credentials, as they don't often like being told by their coach that this is the "only" answer.

Avoid doing this and instead you need to concentrate on a different way of coaching. Since we want to learn how to become better coaches by extracting information from your clients, it makes no sense to asked totally closed questions that are really just slightly interactive elements of a lecture, or a rant.

The best form of coaching questioning is not built around the idea of a rhetorical question – instead, it should be built around having a precise and detailed answer that comes from the student. When you ask the question they should have a clear answer waiting for you. This might not seem like coaching but coaching is not training – you train dogs.

In a good coaching environment you want to merely ask testing questions that gets your student thinking of a way out of that situation for themselves. It's why using the rhetorical question is so dangerous in this context.

Make sure that when you ask a question as a coach that you have both the inclination and the opportunity to hear an answer. The answer from the student should then dictate and shape what you are about to say here.

Good coaching is all about making sure you ask questions that will give the opposition lots of think about, and it will then also give them the chance to learn. Never avoid hearing the answers or queries of a client or student as it is bound to be paramount to their learning experience.

As a coach this is all that matters to you, so don't mess around and make sure that you give the students the chance to give you something to actually talk about and something that allows you to shape and relate the answer to their specific needs and requests.

This is going to make your life MUCH easier moving forward as a coach, as it will leave your students feeling far more involved in the process. Many coaches are simply too wrapped up in the success of their strategy and implementing their philosophy over others that the coaching falls to the wayside.

You should have to demonstrate both great listening skills and teaching skills. You should be capable of orating any answer that they need but to do that you have to ask the right kind of questions – this is what many would refer to as a "simple" question.

In the next section we'll be taking a closer look at what this is and why you should be using the on a regular basis in your coaching. For the time being though, you should definitely consider staying with the avoidance of rhetorical questions if you want to coach properly.

# "Simple" Questions

Of course, like anything else, there can be 'simple' questions to ask – the kind of questions that will ensure you aren't waiting around for answers for too long!

Simple questions can be the best way to get a discussion going and a genuine chat amongst you both that will ensure you can do some learning about the mentality and general state of mind of your student.

This might not sound too important but if you take the time to do so, you are far more likely to get a really positive response.

However, asking simple questions takes a lot more than just going "So, how are you?" this isn't the kind of simple question we are referring to. No, what we mean here is that you need to leave the maximum volume of room possible for a student to answer your questions.

They need to be able to get involved via their own inner thinking, meaning that they can work with you to give you some detailed – and personal – answers that should help you give the right kind of coaching back in return.

The reason why this matters so much is quite simple – you have to allow the student to od the learning themselves.

They need to be able to look inside themselves and find their own relevance, their own references. This lets them think independently and means they won't be beholden to you to give them all the answers, making it easier to hit that right mark together.

Of course, coaching has far more to it than just asking the student questions and then letting them find the answer themselves. If that was all you had to do, everyone would be a coach!

You need to offer a light and rather transparent suggestion when coaching, you have to be the one who offers a bit of guidance. Instead of always offering the same guidance and having a specific answer that is the "right" choice you can turn to these simple question and instead totally change the way that people are looking at you.

You should only intrude if they start to waffle off point with their answer, as you are merely there to try and help them see the right answer by choosing the direction of the conversation.

By asking simple and short questions you can have them find the answers on their own whilst helping you give some respectful little insights and intrusions as they go.

You aren't supposed to be the guru, the one with all the answers, you merely need to be able to read their own potential and strengths to guide them in the right idea. If your question is simple, the answers will be as well.

This not only will help you move in the right direction in terms of finding a solid answer for what they need to know but it should help avoid the coaching from being too generic. Instead of having some dull curriculum that you hand out marks over, proper coaching is all about coaching that specific person.

This means closely listening to their needs and what they need to improve upon to give them the best chance of finding an out.

Just like any other kind of question, a good simple question will be able to give an interesting little insight that they may not have otherwise considered.

# Making Simple Questions Matter

It would be easy to look at what is being said here and imply that you merely just need to give people questions to answer and they will be experts in no time.

This is not what I am trying to say – it's a major part of coaching, but you have to be able to ask the *right* question. Whilst there is no problem in asking a complex question, it has to avoid being complicated i.e. it needs to have an open sense of dialogue, and not feel like you are putting the student into a games show.

If you can do this then you will be far, far more likely to see success moving forward. The major failing of most coaches is simply offering too much of their own insight and asking questions that requires a really specific answer.

This ruins the coaching experience as, if you keep on asking questions that seem complicated, it will seem as if you are trying to overtly challenge or patronize the student – this is probably the worst kind of teaching that you can do. It turns them off your way of thinking entirely.

Instead, make sure that your questions are built not just with a desire to help, but a desire to open up discussion. Fewer, shorter questions is the way to go so you don't feel like you are conducting a police interview.

Never try and make your student feel as if you are trying to trip them up or make them wrong. This creates a negative impact in the room and is likely to weaken the chances of your questions being worth their time answering.

**Tom Mahalo |**

Coaching questions are usually minimalist that try to open up the framework of the students mind, not a question that has a specific or complicated answer. Instead of asking what they think the meaning of life is, asking them what they think the purpose of their own life is.

Whilst never a question likely to come up in any kind of coaching, the difference in wording here is very significant.

One is asking them to talk for the world, which is impossible to answer. The other asks them to talk about themselves, giving you an input into their mentality and thought process.

What one do you think is more likely to succeed?

Now, we're going to take a look at what is known as a neutral question. These are very important for helping to make a solid distinction between asking a question to get information and to help the person and asking a question which looks to deliberately influence or direct the coaching in a direction.

Remember, a good coach can handle any student – you should not have to shape the questioning and the overall coaching on these terms, ever!

The best coaches look to help people on their own personal issues, not lead them down a pre-ordained series of answers.

# Neutral Questions

In this section of the guide, we're going to take a look at what is known as a Neutral question.

This is quite a tough one to get your head around, but the main gist is that the best part about a neutral question is that it dismisses the idea of having an agenda or something similar.

A neutral question is typically built around gaining more information and leading the conversation in a natural direction. You want to learn more, so you have to talk with the person and get used to the way that they are thinking.

Not only does this open up a far more cohesive field of discussion moving forward, but it presents a much better way for you to start defining and eventually controlling emotions without having any specific focus you want to try and touch on.

Neutral questions are good when you still need to discern what the right plan of action should be for your client.

You want to try and open up the discussion with this form of questioning and the best way to do that is to investigate what the student themselves feels about something – "What is your opinion of…" or "How are you feeling about…." Can be a good way to get the conversation moving naturally.

Remember, a good neutral question holds no agenda and does not look to move the discussion in any particular direction.

No, with a neutral question you are more being able to get something simplistic out of the person without halting the chance of debate. Your question has to come without any kind of agenda along the way and they should be used to propose an authentic way of discussion.

Too many coaches look to "ask" questions that merely look to have the student accept their ideas and agree. As far as coaching goes there are few worse options that you could be operating with.

A neutral question is very important as it should be used to search for information and allow the student to dictate what they tell you.

Instead of asking "Don't you?" why not ask "How do you?" it's a simple correction of the terms but it does a major element for helping the discussion to become far more comfortable for both members of the discussion.

A question that is neutral means that it has no agenda, so leave your loaded questions in your head!

## Leading with Neutrality

Of course, a good coach is also capable of offering insight and suggestion into what is being discussed here. It's not about just asking them easy questions and letting them talk it out, as we said before.

No, the aim of a real coach is quite simple – you will be looking to ask a question that allows for you to show your coaching expertise and your intellect, but only when needed.

If you find that the neutral questions are simply not directing the conversation enough and you aren't learning anything, you can take the lead a little bit more without pushing the boundaries totally into having the student just agree with what you have said.

What you can do instead of this is quite simple – you can ask a question that allows to get a specific response to a question whilst allowing them to be open about it.

Rather than suggesting they feel X or Y emotion, you can find out how they feel exactly. "Does that make you…" is a good way to get the person talking properly. It allows you to find out how they feel about a certain subject or event – happiness, sadness, anger etc. – whilst allowing you to confirm or deny any preconceptions you have in your mind.

This means that the client can concentrate on a specific part of the topic whilst still have free reign to discuss other elements on it. Make sure that your leading question does not take precedence over the others.

However they answer your question, ask them about how they truly felt and get them to divulge a little.

This makes it much easier for you to get the answer that you were looking for whilst framing the discussion around what you need. This allows the questions to be neutral – without a particular agenda – whilst letting you gather the information that you need.

Neutral questions should make up a large chunk of your questioning when it comes to coaching as it allows you to find out more about how that person actually feels about it themselves.

This kind of information is absolutely invaluable and will play a massive role in deciding whether you succeed or fail moving forward. Just remember that you are not here to tell them how they feel or what agenda they should be following – it's all about asking questions they can answer.

Next, we're going to look at how dangerous it can be if you allow your level of questioning to revert into an interrogation. You have to be able to make sure that you are asking positive questions, questions that invoke the right kind of thinking about the student, rather than always asking negative questions.

'Do' is more powerful than 'Don't' in coaching as people respond far more actively to a positive line of questioning. We'll help you understand if you are making a major mistake talking to your students in a particular manner, and if you can rectify that mistake.

# **The Threat of Interrogation**

Without a doubt, one of the most common problems that I see within coaches is that they go down the interrogation route. They treat their clients like it's a police interview, asking them questions that seem to be more threatening than helpful. Being a good coach is all about being able to give people a way to express themselves and to answer your questions without making them feel as if they are in the middle of an interview.

If you stray too seriously with your ideas and your interpretations then you can quickly make people feel quite uncomfortable and unsteady in your presence. If you would like to avoid this from becoming a problem them you have to appreciate that the threat of interrogation is a very real problem for most questions.

Instead of starting your questions with negative sounding beginnings such as "Why aren't you…" or "What stops you from…" then you are on the wrong path as a coach. This makes people feel quite uncomfortable with their plan and their way forward, and it actually changes the entire tone of what you were discussing before you got to this point in the coaching, throwing everything that came before it.

Why?

Because you have just made the client start to worry and think about their weaknesses and their negatives. As we mentioned before, the power of good coaching is using your ability to help people see what their attributes are for positive good. If you keep highlighting the things that hold them back and made them feel inadequate then you have just flattened any chance of making cohesive progress.

You should always try and go down a more positive kind of questioning, as hitting people with too many questions of this kind is going to really hamper your chances of being a success within that particular coaching circuit.

Negative questions are very poor questions for a coach to be asking for the large part, as it merely focuses on the mind on what has gone wrong. A strong coach will keep a student's mind towards where they've been successful.

*This is something I have felt personally in the past. I worked with a client who was a very keen learner but who had major self-confidence issues. They believed that they had no right to be involved in the world of business and that they were simply not smart enough for it.*

*Instead of digging deep to find what they did like about themselves, I wanted to know more about what they hated about themselves. Whilst exploring a personality is a much needed trait of a good coach who wants to try and make a difference to the mindset of the client, it can be the easiest way to lead them down a dark path thinking about themselves here.*

Would you like to avoid that? Then you have to start considering what the options are, and what a more progressive way of coaching is going to be for your students.

## Open Ended Questioning

Probably the best way to go about asking questions of this kind to a client is going to come from being open ended and asking questions that have a more positive nature to them. Hitting someone with the same negative questioning without any kind of positive note at the end will leave them sorely concentrating on the thing about themselves that they hate the most.

Want to avoid this and want to keep them feeling good about themselves, always moving forward with the quality and consistency of their thinking? Then consider the positives of using open ended questioning.

Typically, open ended questioning will leave a client with a far more expressive answer to give. It lets you learn about them but it also means you stray away from leaving them with negatives to talk about. Strong, effective open ended questioning is all about giving them something to think about in terms of what makes them strong and worth the risk in the first place.

It helps them break away from the negative stereotypes that permeates their minds and instead allows them to just concentrate on giving you answers about the positives. Open questions allow them to think for themselves, too, though, which is the best element of a good coach.

You aren't expected to deliver any kind of solid answer to them but you aren't supposed to send them on a negative thinking spiral. There is nothing wrong with learning about the weaknesses of the person but there is a lot wrong with asking questions that make them only concentrate on where they have gone wrong.

As a coach, it is your job to let them both talk for themselves and then give them a positive start. Base the conversation around letting them answer questions at length, and base the questions around ways that will help them find their own strengths and weaknesses as they talk.

Try and frame the debate around asking them things like "What choices can you make?" or "What's the next step?" as it makes them think of it for themselves. When you are merely looking for one and only one answer in any kind of coaching you are merely training them in learning specific answers. You aren't letting them learn about situations, which is the domain of a good and clear coach who knows exactly what they are doing.

Remember that your job here is to help them become a more cohesive and confident person so they can use what you do teach them as a coaching lesson. Make them feel on an intellectual par with you by opening up the questions to let them find the answer for themselves. When you do this you are far more likely to see a positive response to the kind of debates that you are having at that moment in time.

So now you can see the great power of open ended questioning and helping to frame your coaching in a positive manner, let's look at something else that is deeply progressive and powerful within coaching – Neurolinguistics.

# !!! BONUS !!! What is Neurolinguistic Programming?

Neurolinguistic Programming – or NLP as we'll be referring to it as – is easily one of the most powerful ways forward for you.

Famous for its elite range of techniques that you can put into active use when using NLP, it has become a system that has become majorly important for many people.

Tom Mahalo |

It's a range of multiple techniques that can be used to help people who are looking to become better coaches, allowing you to frame the level and quality of discussion the way that you would need to so that you can find out the answers you need.

Of course, many are wary of things like NLP. When you speak to a medical professional their own opinion could put you off, as many see NLP as nothing more than pseudoscience.

With that being the case, if managed in the right way then you can quite easily change and alternate the way that your coaching is viewed both by students and even yourself!

However, many are simply too wary of getting involved with something like NLP as they are too scared to find out what power it might hold. As a coach you should never discount on anything that could potentially help both you and your clients

**Tom Mahalo |**

get into the best bracket of results, so why would you ever discount the idea of NLP?

Forget what you've been told before – I know from personal experience that NLP can play a major benefit to a coach if they use it in the right manner.

In the next section we'll be taking a look at some of the best NLP techniques out there, but you have to understand that coaching with NLP is a very hard thing to do.

**What is NLP, Exactly?**

This is something that many don't actually know and this can actively hamper their chances of making a positive and telling impact when using NLP within their own coaching structure.

It started in the late 1960s and was brought to life by the brilliant Richard Bandler. Bandler was a high-end computer scientist undergrad from the University of California.

He had a deep interest in psychotherapy and over time these two interests began to blend together and create a really smart range of ideas that could make a major difference in the near future.

Having noticed the deep level of ineffectiveness of many therapists, he noticed that both Virginia Satir and Fritz Perls were beginning to get far more consistent and telling results than others.

Together with his colleague John Grinder, they closely studied what both therapists were upto and noticed that they both worked with a specific structure to their teachings.

From this teaching and learning, both Bandler and Grinder created what we know of today as NLP.

They also studied the famous hypnotherapist, Milton Erickson. They used both blends of his approach as well as the approach of Satir and Perls. This fine combination was the first beginning of a new therapeutic model, which today we all refer to as NLP.

## NLP Principles

To make the most of NLP you have to first understand what makes it "tick" in the first place. This is the hardest part for many, as it becomes increasingly difficult to understand the major elements that make NLP so effective. The main principles are built around the following ideals;

People are not their behavior. This means that disliking someone because of how they behave is ridiculous and deeply weakens your social and educational pool. When you finally accept someone for who they are, it becomes much easier to alter and change the behavior of both themselves and you.

NLP also believes that every individual already has the capacity to succeed and achieve any outcome on this planet. The main challenge is that most people never investigate or learn how to activate and empower this part of their lives. When they learn how to do this, the parameters for success – and the challenges – will change entirely.

This form of therapy is based around the fact that success comes from communicating with one another. When you communicate with someone, what you respond with to them is going to be heavily determined by the response that you first received from them. If you learn how to communicate and handle the responses that you get, then you will find that the world responds to you in a better way as well.

The final major principle of NLP is that it's rooted in the ability of changing our minds. Solid and rigid thinking is dangerous and greatly limits the potential that we can make of our lives and therefore limits just how successful we can be in many different ways. This is a really important element within NLP as it's decided entirely by how open minded you will decide to be in your life.

If you learn how to manage this aspect of your future then NLP is going to be a major boost for you. However, making the most of the various NLP principles is much easier said than done.

Today, this has become a majorly important system for helping people learn and change.

But for you, as a coach, it could be the most powerful "secret weapon" that you have ever had! It can help you change the way that students deal and cope with their emotions and also how they decide to think about the next step in any plan.

Getting used to this aspect of NLP is very important as a failure to do so means that many will never appreciate what it can do for them. It can be the perfect coaching tool because if it's used in the right manner you'll find that it's much easier to get the coaching to be successful.

Many people need coaching as they have rigid minds and aren't ready to accept an alternative viewpoint or a view of doings things. With NLP you remove this problem and can make it much easier for people to learn.

## Neurolinguistic Programming Techniques

In this final section of the book, we'll be taking a closer look at what makes the world of NLP so hard to master and understand.

For many people it can be a tough thing to get their heads around because it's all about things that go on in the mind – until it "works" NLP shows no real signs of progression or change.

This is why so many decide to give up with NLP; they feel like it does not actively portray the kind of change they were hoping to see.

If this is your mindset, you're bound to miss out on a glorious system!

NLP takes time because it's literally trying to change the way that you think about the world. As a coach you might need to even consider using these NLP techniques yourself to help you become more comfortable with a different train of thought.

Many coaches think they are open minded until they finally look back and see how they have treated clients in the past.

They look at how similar their suggestions and end results have been when working with other clients and see just how badly they messed up here.

To avoid feeling like this, you have to take the time to understand various NLP techniques.

Taking the time to do this will ensure that you have a far more rounded repertoire that puts you ahead of many other coaches.

Alongside asking the right kind of questions – and avoiding the wrong ones – you'll find that it is now much easier to get the kind of answers that you were hoping for.

It will make it easier to ensure your students can become more open minded and more suggestible.

They'll be much more likely to believe in the service that you are offering and the future that may be encased in that.

Not only will it make it much easier for you to make a mark on your coaching, but NLP will have a prominent change in any of the students who undergo it with you.

Try and master the following NLP techniques for your students;

**Take a Literal Stance**

The first – and most useful – of all of our NLP techniques is that you have to get involved with taking people more literally. Many people come to coaches because they have a genuine inability to succeed without one. They cannot picture it in their heads as it just seems so impossible.

When someone feels like that it can be pretty hard to talk them around without taking a literal stance on what they are saying. People can find it hard to picture something because they picture it as something they don't want – instead, try and get your student to picture it as something that they do want to get.

Let's say you're coaching someone on how to get a girlfriend. They most likely look at it as "I don't want to be single anymore!" but instead, get them saying "I want a partner" – positivity creates success.

**Empower with Visualization**

Another great NLP technique is to help people actually see what they want. We discussed above about how some people can struggle to ever get success because they simply cannot picture it happening to them – how can you ever achieve something without a visual representation of that success?

You have to help them visualize it yourself. This is easier said than done, obviously, but it can be made much simpler if you simply take a more literal approach to it. If they cannot see it you have to paint the picture for them. The most common version of this that I have dealt with personally was with my young nephew.

He was desperate to play for his local school football team, but couldn't ever see himself playing. I had to help him work on the things that he was missing from his game at school level (an ability to concentrate basically!) and this really helped both him and myself.

By helping him actually visualize walking out for the local school district tournament, he finally went on to achieve that dream. It took many months of helping him "see" it in his head, but it 100% worked.

He's now the team captain!

**Finding Inner Desire**

A great way to build up a strong NLP platform with your student is to help them look at what their present circumstances are, and how they can move them towards something more desirable.

The problem is that most students lack the resources – mental or physical – to get there, and it's up to you as the coach to give them an easy way to do just this.

**Tom Mahalo |**

The easiest way route to doing this is quite simple – you need to help them change their state of mind. Get them to open up about the sights and sounds that they associated with where they wish to be.

If they cannot get there themselves, then you can get there for them! As a coach you can put yourself in that position for them, as a state of feeling is infectious. If you are in a positive and upbeat mood then you can pass that on to the person, helping them feel more optimistic with their thinking.

The best way to change your state of mind is to be physically active – jumping up and down is enough to start to alter your state of mind. When you do this you are more likely to find a solution for your student. They are more likely to take your lead and follow your positivity, helping them break down some massive mental barriers.

Of course, you can always fake it. If you can pretend to be in a certain state of mind then you can fool your mental state into going along with it. The power of NLP here comes from simply tricking the mind – get your student to think of a point in their lives that made them feel exceptionally happy, or emotionally complete.

If you also do this, you'll be able to get your student to follow your lead and change their state of mind as well!

This is very useful for helping to change a student who is down in the dumps and can't see a new reality into someone who feels far more upbeat about their chances of success in the future.

**Relax the Student**

The finest way to get NLP to work is to simply make them aware that everything you ask of them, they can do with ease. Whenever you are working with a student you will no doubt notice that they are quite apprehensive about any coaching you're about to go through with them.

Success with you gives them the confidence and control to go and get success elsewhere, as it breeds a wining habit. Finding that your students are not able to loosen up and feel at ease even when you tell them this? Then you can alleviate their stress by telling them a story.

A story will work with them to make them feel more aware about the direction they want to be heading in. Tell those stories that end with you looking like the winner, where you knew what decisions to make, where you felt uber-confident.

Why? Because this rubs off on the person. The student is going to be subconsciously rattling through their memory bank to find a story that fits the same style for them. They might not tell you but inside they are looking for the perfect experience that accurately relates to yours.

Now, ask them to do the same – to relate a story where they felt super confident. It does not have to be their most confident or their finest hour, though, as saying that can add pressure that was not needed. Instead, this helps them relax and removes the added pressure.

However, some will respond to you with polarity. They want to give you their most confident story because you asked them not to – this actually plays into your hands. You want the most confident story but some people just don't feel comfortable enough doing that.

Remove that confusion from the table and instead let them tell the story they feel most comfortable with. Once you do this and you both are rattling with confidence due to telling your stories, transfer that confidence and positive energy into the problems they are having.

The best coaches remove the tension of discussion with a story; become like a bard of old, telling amazing stories, and you can find that your students will be far more comfortable when it comes to tackling their issues. NLP dictates that we can give someone confidence through telling them of our own – it makes them relate to our confidence and, as we mentioned before, the body takes after how we are feeling subconsciously.

You can now send them away feeling uber confident, ready to attack the day and to deal with the problems they dealt with. They won't know why they feel so confident, but it's down to your promoting their ability to feel confident.

**The Conversational Method**

One of the best ways to make a positive change and effective alteration in the life of one of your clients is just to start talking. Not only does this make a fresher more engaging environment to get into NLP with but it helps the student loosen up a little bit.

People seem to think that what they say can be pre-ordained and that it can all be planned.

Explain to them that language is automatic and that our body comes up with the word selection needed to try and articulate what we have to say in response to whatever communication aim we had. If it was to hurt someone's feelings, we'll find a way – or at least, we'll try!

To become a stronger individual it helps to appreciate that our language is assembled with a subconscious goal in mind. Helping your students become more conversationally open, not fearing what their subconscious is going to put together, is so important. We all go through the failure of talking as a child – you just experiment until you finally get "the picture".

The best way to kick this off with a student is just to ask "What happens when you…" and try and relate that into what they need help. Just ask them what happens to them when they achieve the goal you have both set, and watch them have fun! Make them feel fine about making mistakes throughout it, too.

This can take a bit of time to get used to and to master it but the conversional method is a great NLP technique. They'll eventually unwind what their subconscious goals are, helping them both appreciate their talents and also help them appreciate the goals they have started to set.

Start without starting.

What does this mean? You might notice that many people get guarded when you "start". Well, why not make the start a fake one?

This is a strong NLP technique and get you learning more from your students that they may have otherwise not mentioned.

This is very useful as you simply need to turn to the person and state that "Before we begin, I would just like to...." And then actually start.

This makes them more relaxed and far less guarded, allowing you to get in there with the question long before they would have expected you to.

This should strengthen your hand. If you find that this does not work then you can try it the other way. Simply stop the interview and what you were doing, and then give ask the toughest questions when you're "finished"!

**Using NLP**

Once you master these as a coach, each of these has a very useful and effective range of success. They can all be used to help people become more suggestible.

People see the word 'programming' here and think it's some kind of cheap pseudo-mind control, giving people the only one way of looking at things and staying with you along the way.

If this is something that you think NLP is about, you should take the time to re-read this section again!

It's all about helping people be more open-minded with their approach to life and to different solutions they had not considered.

This is more likely to have a lasting positive impression and when used in conjunction with the kind of smart questioning techniques along the way, you'll see major change.

Avoid giving people only one path to go down and you have a much greater chance of being seen as a coach that truly helps people!

# **Conclusion**

As you can see, there is an incredible amount of things to consider about the changes and the overall challenges that lie in wait for you. Coaching is never going to be easy – you are after all about to try and change the thought process, the mentality and the overall belief in someone!

This is a powerful and deeply engaging process to deal with and for many coaches it can simply be too tough to work out. If you want to help get around this then you can use the techniques listed inside for consistent, long-term help.

There is one thing that you should keep in mind moving forward if you want to be the best coach that you can, though. Your questions can be as detailed and well put as you like but if you don't show the requisite level of empathy for the person who is asking for your help, you will never succeed.

Success as a coach comes from being able to show someone the kind of empathy that they need – and deserve. If someone comes to you for help then they likely need you to do something that will change their entire lives!

This is why you have to be ready to dispense out the advice and the help that they need readily, helping them find the problems and then also the solutions. As a coach you have to know what they want and how they wish to achieve it, so that you can ask the questions that helps them move in that direction.

Remember, as a coach you aren't here to simply throw advice at people and command them as if they are a peon. Instead, you are here to help them think through problems and to talk to them, hoping they can find the solutions within themselves instead.

It will take some time to get it right with most patients but you are here to help them find the answers, acting as a passive guide. The best way to do this is with conversation, and the conversation will be framed in the terms that you both decide upon – and in the way that you put your questions forward to the individual.

This will help them really understand and appreciate the way forward, and could be the sole catalyst that you need to start pushing your patients and your students in the right direction.

*Best of luck!*

*Tom Mahalo*